Preface

The field of System Analysis and Design is a foundational element in the world of information systems, serving as the blueprint for developing robust, efficient, and scalable software solutions. As organizations increasingly rely on sophisticated information systems to manage their operations, the demand for professionals skilled in analyzing and designing these systems is at an all-time high. Recognizing the critical importance of this discipline, the Indira Gandhi National Open University (IGNOU) has included System Analysis and Design as a key component of its curriculum, challenging students to acquire both theoretical knowledge and practical skills.

This book, IGNOU System Analysis and Design Previous Years Unsolved Papers (MCS-014), is a carefully curated compilation of unsolved question papers from previous years. It is designed to serve as an essential resource for students preparing for their exams in this subject. The primary objective of this book is to provide students with a comprehensive tool to self-assess their understanding, identify areas for improvement, and enhance their problem-solving abilities.

We believe that practicing with previous years' question papers is one of the most effective ways to prepare for exams. It not only acquaints students with the types and formats of questions they are likely to encounter but also deepens their comprehension of the subject matter by applying theoretical concepts to practical scenarios. By working through these unsolved papers, students will be able to evaluate their readiness, improve their time management during exams, and build confidence in tackling complex questions.

The decision to present the papers unsolved was deliberate. We encourage students to engage actively with the material, think critically, and explore multiple approaches to solving the problems. This method promotes independent learning and ensures that students are well-prepared to adapt to various question formats and levels of difficulty during the actual exams.

This book covers a broad range of topics within System Analysis and Design, including system development life cycle (SDLC), requirement analysis, system design, implementation strategies, and maintenance. Each paper has been meticulously selected to ensure a comprehensive coverage of the syllabus, providing students with a thorough understanding of the core concepts required for success in their exams.

We hope that this book will not only support students in their academic journey but also inspire them to delve deeper into the fascinating field of System Analysis and Design. As technology continues to evolve, the knowledge and skills gained in System Analysis and Design will be instrumental in shaping the future of information systems development.

We would like to extend our gratitude to the faculty members and students of IGNOU who have contributed to the development of this book. Your feedback and insights have been invaluable in ensuring that this book meets the needs of today's learners.

Table of Contents

MCS-014
MCA (Revised) / BCA (Revised)
Chapter 1: Term-End Examination, June, 2010
MCS-014: System Analysis and Design

Time: 3 Hours
Maximum Marks: 100
Weightage: 70

Note: (i) Question No. 1 is compulsory.
(ii) Answer any three Questions from the rest.

1. (a) Draw a data flow diagrams (DFDs) fill 2-levels depicting the various processes, data flow and data repositories for a
"Computer-Institute Management System". Follow the appropriate conventions/ symbols as given in your study material.
10

(b) What kind of fact-finding techniques would you use for investigating the information requirements for a multi-speciality hospital, which is presently doing manual registrations? Which kind of techniques do you think will be more effective? Also,mention the problems you anticipate in conducting the investigations.
10

(c) Explain the role of MIS in an organisation. List and explain different kinds of Information Systems.
1
0

(d) With the help of a diagram explain different components of a typical CASE tool. Also cite certain examples of CASE tools, being used at different SDLC levels.
10

2. (a) Describe the role of a Systems Analyst. Also, list various skills that the Systems Analyst should possess.
10

(b) Identify various reports/outputs/products associated with each and every phase of a SDLC.
10

3. (a) Mention various criteria for the Report design.
10

(b) With the help of a neat diagram discuss various components of Decision Support Systems (DSS).

1

0

4. (a) With reference to Risk Assessment and management, write short notes on the following: 10

i. Quantitative Risk analysis
ii. Qualitative Risk analysis

(b) Explain various issues involved in software maintenance, with appropriate specific examples. 10

5. Write short notes on the following: 5x4=20

a) Knowledge Acquisition by Expert Systems.
b) Disaster recovery.
c) Criteria for form design.
d) System Audit.

MCS-014
MCA (Revised) / BCA (Revised)
Chapter 2: Term-End Examination, December, 2010
MCS-014: System Analysis and Design

Time: 3 Hours
Maximum Marks: 100
Weightage: 70

Note: (i) Question No. 1 is compulsory.
(ii) Answer any three Questions from the rest.

1.(a) Construct an Entity Relationship Diagram for employee management system. Also construct a relational database schema for it.
10

(b) With the help of diagrams, explain the steps in physical and logical design.
10

(c) What are the CASE tools? Explain object-oriented CASE tools in detail. Also explain differentiate between Reverse and forward engineering.
10

(d) Describe the various levels and components of MIS. Explain the role of a system analyst in system development.
10

2. (a) Develop a SRS for inventory management system. Give any three characteristics of SRS.
8

(b) Why is feasibility study considered an important task in system development? Classify feasibility and elaborate the key features of each.
8

(c) Classify Information systems and describe the characterizing features, in brief.
4

3. (a) Explain in brief, the following SDLC models (suitable diagrams):
4x2=8
(i) Waterfall Model. (With feedback
(ii) Spiral Model.
Explain the key features of the above models.

(b) What are the various types of documentation. Give an example of each type.
6

(c) Differentiate between a decision tree and a decision table. Give an example and explain the decision table.
6

4. (a) Give steps in Report design. Classify Reports.
6

(b) Write short notes on the following:
4x2=8
(i) JAD
(ii) data dictionary

(c) Why is audit important for system development. Explain the types of audits.
6.

5. (a) What is cost Benefit analysis. Explain one model with a suitable example.
8

(b) What are the various types of file organisation? Describe in brief.
4

(c) Differentiate between various types of coupling and cohesion. Which of these types (in each) is the best and worst and why?
8

MCS-014
MCA (Revised) / BCA (Revised)
Chapter 3: Term-End Examination, June, 2011
MCS-014: System Analysis and Design

Time: 3 Hours
Maximum Marks: 100
Weightage: 70

Note: (i) Question No. 1 is compulsory.
(ii) Answer any three Questions from the rest.

1. (a) Construct a data flow diagram (level 0 and 1) for a library management system. Also draw the respective ERDs for it.
10

(b) Explain the steps and activities in the design phase, of SDLC.
10

(c) Explain the key features of the followings:
10

(i) Prototyping Model
(ii) Spiral Model

Give a brief note on system maintenance and explain any 1 model of system maintenance (with a diagram).

(d) What is the importance of security and protection of databases for any organisation? What are the various policies and methods to ensure security of databases?
10

2. (a) Explain the key players and their roles and responsibilities at various levels of a MIS. Explain the tasks performed at DSS in detail.
10

(b) Differentiate between a decision table and a decision tree. Prepare a sample data dictionary for an employee management system.
8

(c) Prepare a brief note on user documentation, as well as utility.
2

3. (a) What is cost estimation? Give one model used by an organisation for cost benefit analysis.
7

(b) Explain the essential features of a SRS and prepare it for a project on 'Student Enrollment System'.
7

(c) Write a brief note on an 'expert system and its key characteristics'.
6

4. (a) Give differences between internal information and turnaround information. Also describe the process of designing a form.
8

(b) What is denormalization? Give a suitable example to explain it. Also explain the process of denormalization of tables.
6

(c) Differentiate between various types of databases and differentiate between a DBMS and a file-system.
6

5. Write short notes on the following with example of each:
5x4=20

(a) Information System Design
(b) Modularity
(c) System testing
(d) CASE tools

MCS-014
MCA (Revised) / BCA (Revised)
Chapter 4: Term-End Examination, June, 2012
MCS-014: System Analysis and Design

Time: 3 Hours
Maximum Marks: 100
Weightage: 70

Note: (i) Question No. 1 is compulsory.
(ii) Answer any three Questions from the rest.

1. (a) What are different phases in SDLC? What is need of System Analysis? Explain the role of System Analyst.
10

(b) Draw a Data Flow Diagram (DFD) till second level Depicting the various processes, data flow and data repositories for a "Petrol - Pump retail outlet".
10

(c) What is meant by "System Design Specification"? Explain the purpose of the following system design tools:
9
(i) Object Interaction Diagram
(ii) Inheritance Diagram
(iii) Aggregation Diagram

(d) What is DSS? Explain various components briefly with the help of a suitable diagram.
6

(e) What is reverse engineering? Explain the need of reverse engineering with an example.
5

2. (a) What are object-oriented Case Tools? List basic features of OO Case Tools. Also write differences between various types of OO Case Tools.
10

(b) What is on - line transaction processing? Give an example of on - line transaction processing. Also differentiate between on - line transaction, processing and batch processing.
10

3. (a) What is transaction audit? Explain four advantages of transaction audit.
10

(b) What is Joint Application Development GAD)? Explain six typical participants in a JAD.
10

4. (a) What is need of software testing? Describe the objectives of the following testing techniques: 10

a) Stress Testing
b) Performance Testing
c) Recovery Testing
d) Security Testing

(b) What is need of standard software documentation? Explain any three documentation standards briefly.

5. (a) Briefly, discuss various criteria for Form and Report design, using an example.
10

(b) Write a short note on following:
5x2=10
(i) Coupling and cohesion
(ii) Distributed system

MCS-014
MCA (Revised) / BCA (Revised)
Chapter 5: Term-End Examination, December, 2012
MCS-014: System Analysis and Design

Time: 3 Hours
Maximum Marks: 100
Weightage: 70

Note: (i) Question No. 1 is compulsory.
(ii) Answer any three Questions from the rest.

1. (a) List the underlying principles for a prototype design. Under which conditions, this design will be useful? With the help of an example system, explain its approach.
10

(b) Draw a data flow diagram (DFD) till second level, depicting various processes, data flow and data repositories for a "Study centre Management System". Follow appropriate conventions/ symbols as were given in your study material.
10

(c) Explain what kind of fact-finding techniques would you use for deciding on the design of a new application/system for some "Assignments Management System" at a study centre.
10

(d) Explain briefly the criteria for the following:
10
(i) Form Design
(ii) Report Design

2. (a) Define a Decision Support System (DSS). What are its characteristics? Also list and explain various components of DSS.
10

(b) Explain Reverse and Forward Engineering with the help of an example for each.
10

3. (a) Define Internal Information. Where is it useful? Also discuss various sub classes of internal information with the help of an example for each.
10

(b) What is Cohesion? Explain any four types of Cohesion.
10

4. (a) List and explain the Goals of a Good Design. Also discuss as set of guidelines to be followed basing upon the good design.
10

(b) Explain various steps involved in the process of documentation.
10

5. Write short notes on the following:
4x5=20

(a) Data Dictionary
(b) Joint Application Development
(c) Cost Benefit Analysis
(d) Any two types of system testing.

MCS-014
MCA (Revised) / BCA (Revised)
Chapter 6: Term-End Examination, June, 2013
MCS-014: System Analysis and Design

Time: 3 Hours
Maximum Marks: 100
Weightage: 70

Note: (i) Question No. 1 is compulsory.
(ii) Answer any three Questions from the rest.

1. (a) Draw a Data Flow Diagram (DFD) till second level depicting various processes, data flow and data repositories for a "Library Management System". Follow the conventions.
10

(b) Define a Structure Chart. Draw a Structure Chart for a Payroll Processing System. Also, explain the symbols used in the chart.
10

(c) Define modularity. Describe the ways and means to achieve modularity. Explain with the help of an example.
10

(d) Write the importance of quality in software development. List specifications of various quality factors.
10

2. (a) Explain Real Time Systems and Distributed Systems.
10

(b) Explain Structured Analysis and Structured Design. What are its goals?
10

3. (a) What are the various activities involved in the feasibility study? Discuss any three feasibilities need to be studied during feasibility analysis.
10

(b) What are top-down design and bottom-up approaches? Design top-down approach for any system of your choice.
10

4. (a) Describe all the steps involved in database design for the system discussed in 1 (a) question.
10

(b) Define CASE tools. Explain their role.
5

(c) With the help of an example, explain a sequence diagram.
5

5. Write short notes on the following:
4x5=20

(a) Participatory Design
(b) Test Design Document
(c) Coupling
(d) Decision Tables

MCS-014
MCA (Revised) / BCA (Revised)
Chapter 7: Term-End Examination, December, 2013
MCS-014: System Analysis and Design

Time: 3 Hours
Maximum Marks: 100
Weightage: 70

Note: (i) Question No. 1 is compulsory.
(ii) Answer any three Questions from the rest.

1. (a) Explain how both waterfall model and prototyping model can be accommodated in the spiral process model.
10

(b) A program is to be developed to simulate the operations of a scientific calculator. List the facilities to be provided by this
calculator. Analyze this using a DFD 0 - level and 1 - level diagram.
10

(c) Give full form of CASE. Draw CASE diagram showing all components. Describe each component briefly.
6

(d) Distinguish between Analysis and Design. Explain with example.
10

(e) Explain the following terms:
2x2=4
(i) Debugging
(ii) Cost - Benefit Analysis.

2. (a) Draw ER diagram for the following situation:
6
An account is a relationship between a customer and a bank. A customer has a name. A bank has a branch. A customer may have several accounts of different types and balance.

(b) Describe characteristics of a good interface. List some guidelines to design output screens, icons and graphics.
8

(c) Why is documentation important to information system life cycle? Explain. Also describe the term program specification in brief. What information does it convey?
6

3. (a) Explain the term 'Expert System'. Briefly explain the characteristics of an expert system. Give an example.
8

(b) Why is maintenance of a software important? Discuss some of the problems that are faced during maintenance of software.
6

(c) Differentiate between software Re-engineering and software Reverse Engineering. Explain their need with suitable examples.
6

4. (a) Explain the difference between a structured interview and an unstructured interview? When is each type of interview appropriately used?
6

(b) Explain the following (with an example).
6

(i) Inheritance Diagram
(ii) Aggregation Diagram

(c) Prepare SRS for an "Inventory Management System" for a retail medical store. Also explain the Risk assessment and
management in brief. Make necessary assumptions.
8

5. (a) Explain various types of file organization. Differentiate between a master file and a transaction file.
6

(b) Differentiate between the following: 4x2=8
(i) Batch and Online Transaction Processing.
(ii) TPS and DSS

(c) Describe the aims and methodology of the following testing techniques: 3x2=6
(i) Black Box Testing
(ii) White Box Testing

MCS-014
MCA (Revised) / BCA (Revised)
Chapter 8: Term-End Examination, June, 2014
MCS-014: System Analysis and Design

Time: 3 Hours
Maximum Marks: 100
Weightage: 70

Note: (i) Question No. 1 is compulsory.
(ii) Answer any three Questions from the rest.

1. (a) What type of projects are amenable for Spiral model? Justify your answer with an example.
8

(b) Explain the characteristics of an Information System in detail.
8

(c) Consider a software which registers students for different programmes. The students fill a form and submit it. This is sent to the departments for confirmation. Once it is confirmed, the form and the fees is sent to the account section. Draw a DFD 1 - level and 2 - level for development of software mentioned.
8

(d) Differentiate between function-oriented design and object-oriented design. Also, explain the problems which arise if two modules have high coupling.
8

(e) Explain various criteria and specifications to be considered while designing forms and Reports.
8

2. (a) List any five fact finding techniques for system study and explain any two of them in detail. Differentiate between these two with respect to their merits and demerits.
10

(b) Explain the characteristics of MIS. Give the components of MIS. Also differentiate between DSS and expert system.8

(c) Give an example of a structure chart and explain it.
2

3. (a) Distinguish between technical, operational and economic feasibility with suitable examples.
4

(b) Prepare SRS for 'Airline Reservation System.' Make assumptions wherever necessary.
8

(c) What are the roles of a system analyst in system development? What is a data dictionary? Mention the uses of data dictionary by a system analyst, with the help of an example. Explain the contents of data dictionaries.

8

4. (a) What is a Test Design Document? Explain the contents of this document.

8

(b) Differentiate between the following:

2x2=4

(i) Flat files and Database

(ii) System Testing and Unit Testing

(c) Categorise CASE tools. Give a diagram to explain various components of a CASE tool.

8

5. (a) Give short notes on:

3x3=9

(i) Transaction Audit

(ii) Types of Coupling

(iii) Decision Trees.

(b) What is the need of functional decomposition in software development? Explain with an example.

5

(c) Explain the concept of Information Security and its architecture. Write a short note on threats and risks in a system.

6

MCS-014
MCA (Revised) / BCA (Revised)
Chapter 9: Term-End Examination, December, 2014
MCS-014: System Analysis and Design

Time: 3 Hours
Maximum Marks: 100
Weightage: 70

Note: (i) Question No. 1 is compulsory.
(ii) Answer any three Questions from the rest.

1. (a) What is an Information System? Explain classification of systems in brief. Also explain the need of SDLC for proper development of a system.
10

(b) What is SRS? Briefly explain any four characteristics of SRS. Develop an SRS for Library Management System. Make appropriate assumptions.
10

(c) What is coupling? Explain advantages and disadvantages of a highly coupled system.
5

(d) Explain basic guidelines for user interface design.
5

(e) What is the need of documentation in System Development? Explain, in brief, any two categories of documentation.
5

(f) What is CASE tool? Categorise various types of CASE tools.
5

2. (a) What are the various security issues in a computer system? Explain how an organization may prevent security concerns
from data stored in its centralized and distributed databases.
10

(b) What are Forms? Also explain the process of Form design.
10

3. (a) Why is a proper database design essential for a successful information system? Explain rules for designing tables, fields and constraints.
10

(b) What are the advantages of modular system design? Draw a structure chart for Banking Management System.
10

4. (a) What is a decision tree? Draw a decision tree for a system of your choice.
5

(b) What is a flow chart? Draw a flow chart to find the average marks of of the 10 students in a batch at a study centre.
5

(c) What is the need of system maintenance? Explain different types of maintenance.
10

5. Write short notes on the following:
4x5=20
(a) Expert System
(b) Prototyping Model
(c) Decision Table
(d) System Testing

MCS-014
MCA (Revised) / BCA (Revised)
Chapter 10: Term-End Examination, June, 2015
MCS-014: System Analysis and Design

Time: 3 Hours
Maximum Marks: 100
Weightage: 70

Note: (i) Question No. 1 is compulsory.
(ii) Answer any three Questions from the rest.

1. (a) What is the role of a system analyst in system development? Explain any six attributes of a good system analyst.
8

(b) What is modularity? How can modularity in design be achieved? Explain the advantages of modular design.
10

(c) What is MIS? What are the various functions of MIS in a business organization?
6

(d) What is the need of feasibility study of an information system? Explain the different operational feasibility issues of a system.
8

(e) What is database design? Explain the different issues involved in the designing of a database.
8

2. (a) What is cost and effort estimation.? Give a - brief explanation of any cost and effort estimation model.
8

(b) What is decision table? Design a decision table for Library Management System. Make appropriate assumptions.
8

(c) Explain the responsibility and authority of the system auditor.
4

3. (a) What is DFD 7 Draw a DFD (0 and 1 level) for Online Admission System to offer online admission to graduate and post graduate students of a university.
10

(b) Explain the steps and activities in the testing and maintenance phases of SDLC.
10

4. (a) What is Decision Support System (DSS)? What are its basic characteristics? Briefly explain the various components of DSS, with the help of a diagram.
10

(b) Draw the object interaction diagram for a system of your choice.
5

(c) What is a report? Briefly explain the criteria for report design.
5

5. Write short notes on the following:
4x5=20

(a) Software Quality Assurance
(b) CASE Tools
(c) Real Time System
(d) Software Documentation

MCS-014
MCA (Revised) / BCA (Revised)
Chapter 11: Term-End Examination, December, 2015
MCS-014: System Analysis and Design

Time: 3 Hours
Maximum Marks: 100
Weightage: 70

Note: (i) Question No. 1 is compulsory.
(ii) Answer any three Questions from the rest.

1. (a) Draw a 0-level and 1-level DFD of a library information system. Make necessary assumptions.
1
0

(b) Explain the term 'Feasibility study'. Explain the categories of feasibility with suitable examples.
6

(c) Explain waterfall model with the help of a diagram. How is it different from spiral model? Explain the merits and demerits of both the models.
10

(d) Differentiate between various types of file organisations.
4

(e) Explain the term MIS. Explain the components of a transaction processing system with suitable diagram.
10

2. (a) Construct an Entity Relationship diagram for an airlines reservation system.
8

(b) What is meant by the term CASE? Describe the various components and tools of CASE.
8

(c) Explain the terms 'User manual' and `System documentation'.
4

3. (a) What is the relevance of an Information Security Architecture in MIS? Draw its diagram.
8

(b) Differentiate between System Analysis and System Design. What are the issues and constraints to be taken care of while designing a software product?
8

(c) Differentiate between Reverse engineering and Forward engineering. What is meant by a legacy system?
4

4. (a) Prepare SRS for a "University admission system". Make necessary assumptions.
8

(b) Differentiate between coupling and cohesion. Explain the various types of coupling.
8

(c) What is meant by "User Interface"? What are the basic guidelines to design a user interface?
4

5. (a) What are the essential criteria for form design and report design? Explain.
8

(b) Explain software maintenance and differentiate between various types of software maintenance.
8

(c) Give any one method of cost benefit analysis and explain it. 4

MCS-014
MCA (Revised) / BCA (Revised)
Chapter 12: Term-End Examination, June, 2016
MCS-014: System Analysis and Design

Time: 3 Hours
Maximum Marks: 100
Weightage: 70

Note: (i) Question No. 1 is compulsory.
(ii) Answer any three Questions from the rest.

1. (a) Prepare SRS for a library management system. Make necessary assumptions. 8

(b) Draw ERD for a library management system. Explain various components and relationships in detail. 8

(c) Differentiate between DFD and Flow chart. Discuss the importance of levels of DFD. 8

(d) Explain the following diagrams with examples:
2x4=8
(i) Structured chart
(ii) State-machine diagram

(e) What are the guidelines for database design? Explain the term 'Relational Database Schema'. Give an example of this schema.
8

2. (a) Differentiate between Software Re-engineering and Reverse engineering. 8

(b) Draw a decision table and a decision tree for a problem statement of your choice. Make necessary assumptions. 8

(c) What is meant by 'Expert System'? Why is it required? Give its features. 4

3. (a) What are the components of a MIS? Differentiate between DSS and TPS. Also explain various components of TPS in detail.
8

(b) Explain various types of cohesion. Give an example of a cohesion module. Explain. 8

(c) Explain any three fact finding techniques. Give their merits and demerits. 4

4. (a) What is a 'User Interface'? Explain the guidelines for designing a user interface. 8

(b) Differentiate between various concurrent audit techniques explaining their merits and features. 6

(c) What are the various standards of documentation? Also, explain in brief, the various components of software user documentation. 6

5. (a) Explain the differences between functional testing and structural testing. 8

(b) What are the various steps in logical design? Explain the use of normalization in database design. 8

(c) Explain the responsibilities of a system analyst. Give any two essential qualifications of a system analyst. 4

MCS-014
MCA (Revised) / BCA (Revised)
Chapter 13: Term-End Examination, December, 2016
MCS-014: System Analysis and Design

Time: 3 Hours
Maximum Marks: 100
Weightage: 70

Note: (i) Question No. 1 is compulsory.
(ii) Answer any three Questions from the rest.

1. (a) Draw a Data Flow Diagram (DFD) from context level till second level clearly showing various processes, data flow and data repositories for a "Library Management System".
10

(b) Define 'Modularity'. Write any two goals of a good design. Also write at least four guidelines for achieving the goals mentioned.
10

(c) Explain how both waterfall model and prototyping model can be accommodated in the spiral model.
1
0

(d) Explain relational, hierarchical and network models of database design, with examples.
10

2. (a) Describe the characteristics of a good interface. List some guidelines to design output screens, icons and graphics.
10

(b) What is an E-R diagram? Construct an E-R diagram for a "Railway Reservation System". Make necessary assumptions.
10

3. (a) Prepare an outline of SRS for a "Railway Reservation System". Make suitable assumptions wherever necessary.
10

(b) Define the term 'Cohesion'. Explain any two types of cohesion.
10

4. (a) Explain any two ways of Requirements Gatherings. What are their shortcomings? Use examples to explain.
10

(b) Define the term "Decision Support System". Explain its various components.
10

5. (a) What is a Form? What are the advantages of having forms as part of user interface? What are the criteria used for Form Design?
10

(b) How does Reverse Engineering differ from Forward Engineering? Explain with example.
10

MCS-014

MCA (Revised) / BCA (Revised)

Chapter 14: Term-End Examination, June, 2017

MCS-014: System Analysis and Design

Time: 3 Hours
Maximum Marks: 100
Weightage: 70

Note: (i) Question No. 1 is compulsory.
(ii) Answer any three Questions from the rest.

1. (a) Draw a Data Flow Diagram (DFD) from context level till second level clearly showing various processes, data flow and data repositories for a "Student Information System".
10

(b) What is meant by "Joint Application Development"? Who are the participants in it? What are their roles? Explain briefly.
10

(c) Explain any five fact finding techniques along with their advantages and disadvantages.
10

(d) What is a CASE tool? Explain the various components of a CASE tool with the help of a diagram.
1
0

2. (a) What is the need for Documentation? Draw a diagram depicting various stages of the process of Documentation.
10

(b) What is the role of a Systems Analyst? Explain any two skills that are required to be a Systems Analyst.
10

3. (a) How does a structure chart differ from a flow chart?" Draw a structure chart for a "Student Information System". Make necessary assumptions.
10

(b) How does an E-R diagram differ from a DFD? Draw an E-R diagram for a "Student Information System". Make necessary assumptions.
10

4. (a) What is an Expert System? Give an example of an Expert System. What are its features? Explain the risks associated with its use.
10

(b) Prepare an outline of SRS for a "Student Information System". Make necessary assumptions. 10

5. (a) What do you mean by Information Security? Write a short note on Threats and Risks in a system. 10

(b) What is MIS? How is it useful for management control and strategic planning in an organization? 10

MCS-014

MCA (Revised) / BCA (Revised)
Chapter 15: Term-End Examination, December, 2017
MCS-014: System Analysis and Design

Time: 3 Hours
Maximum Marks: 100
Weightage: 70

Note: (i) Question No. 1 is compulsory.
(ii) Answer any three Questions from the rest.

1. (a) List the underlying principles for a prototype design. Under which conditions will this design be useful? With the help of an example system, explain its approach.
10

(b) Draw a 0-level and 1-level DFD of a "Library Information System". Make necessary assumptions.
1
0

(c) Draw ERD for a "Library Information System". Make necessary assumptions.
10

(d) Assume that an organization does not implement MIS. However, after a couple of years, it decides to implement it. What
problems do you anticipate in implementing MIS in an organization which did not implement it earlier? How would you handle them?
10

2. (a) Define a "Decision Support System (DSS)". What are its characteristics? Also, list and explain various components of a DSS.
10

(b) Define CASE. Explain its various components and tools. Give any two examples of CASE tools.
1
0

3. (a) Develop SRS outline for a "Library Information System". Make necessary assumptions.
10

(b) Explain the five types of system testing.
10

4. (a) Explain the process of designing Forms and Reports.
10

(b) Explain any five different fact finding techniques.
10

5. Write short notes on the following:
(a) Different Standards for Documentation
10

(b) Audit of Transactions on Computer
10

MCS-014
MCA (Revised) / BCA (Revised)
Chapter 16: Term-End Examination, June, 2018
MCS-014: System Analysis and Design

Time: 3 Hours
Maximum Marks: 100
Weightage: 70

Note: (i) Question No. 1 is compulsory.
(ii) Answer any three Questions from the rest.

1. (a) Draw a 0-level and 1-level DFD of a "Grade Card Generation System for a University". Make necessary assumptions.
10

(b) Draw an ERD for a "Grade Card Generation System for a University". Make necessary assumptions.
1
0

(c) Write SRS outline for "Grade Card Generation System for a University". Make necessary assumptions.
10

(d) Explain various approaches for development of information systems.
10

2. (a) What do you mean by "Feasibility Study"? Explain different types of feasibility studies.
10

(b) With the help of an example, explain different types of fields in a table. Also, explain rules for naming tables and fields.
10

3. (a) Explain different types of maintenance activities of a software system.
10

(b) Explain the differences between various types of Object-oriented CASE Tools.
10

4. (a) Define the term "Data Dictionary". Give an example.
10

(b) Why do analysts use data dictionaries? List the reasons.
10

5. Write a short note on the following:

(a) Real Time Systems and Distributed Systems
10

(b) Cost-Benefit Analysis
10

MCS-014
MCA (Revised) / BCA (Revised)
Chapter 17: Term-End Examination, December, 2018
MCS-014: System Analysis and Design

Time: 3 Hours
Maximum Marks: 100
Weightage: 70

Note: (i) Question No. 1 is compulsory.
(ii) Answer any three Questions from the rest.

1. (a) Explain the advantages and disadvantages of the following software development models:
9

(i) Waterfall
(ii) Prototype
(iii) Spiral

(b) What are the advantages of DFDs? Draw DFDs of level-0 and level-1 for online examination system in which examinations are conducted using multiple choice questions and true/false questions. Make necessary assumptions.
10

(c) Explain why a system analyst should be familiar with technical skills. Also list any five technical skills which may be used by a system analyst.
6

(d) Explain data coupling with the help of an example.
5

(e) What is an expert system? Explain its two advantages and two disadvantages.
5

(f) What is MIS? Explain any two functions of MIS in a business organization.
5

2. (a) Explain various roles of a system analyst in modern business.
8

(b) Explain the need of feasibility study for the development of an enterprise application system. Explain various issues involved in operational feasibility.
8

(c) What is risk analysis? Explain quantitative risk analysis.
4

3. (a) What is software re-engineering How is it different from software reverse-engineering? Explain the advantages of both.
10

(b) Draw ER Diagram for the following situation:
10

An account is a relationship between Customer and Bank. A customer may have multiple accounts of different types (but
only one account of one type). Each customer belongs to a branch of bank. Different types of accounts require different minimum balances. A customer may transfer money from one account to another account owned by him/her. Make necessary assumptions.

4. (a) Explain the following with an example of each:
2x5=10

(i) Use case diagram
(ii) Class diagram

(b) What is a CASE tool? How are CASE tools useful in different aspects of software engineering projects? Also briefly explain any two disadvantages of CASE tools.
10

5. Write short notes on the following:
4x5=20

(a) Software Maintenance
(b) User Interface Design
(c) Real Time Systems
(d) Software Documentation

MCS-014
MCA (Revised) / BCA (Revised)
Chapter 18: Term-End Examination, June, 2019
MCS-014: System Analysis and Design

Time: 3 Hours **Maximum Marks: 100**
Weightage: 70

Note: (i) Question No. 1 is compulsory.
(ii) Answer any three Questions from the rest.

1. (a) Describe the significance of a Data Flow Diagram (DFD). Draw DFD's upto 2nd level for a Study Centre Management System depicting various processes, data flow and data repositories. Follow all the conventions properly.
10

(b) Describe Open systems and Closed systems. Give two examples for each.
10

(c) What is the role of fact finding techniques in systems development? Mentioning their advantages and disadvantages, explain the following fact finding techniques:
10
(i) Interviews
(ii) Group Discussions

(d) List and explain any two object oriented CASE tools along with a suitable example.
10

2. (a) Describe the following types of maintenance activities: $4x2\frac{1}{2}$=
10
(i) Corrective maintenance
(ii) Adaptive maintenance
(iii) Perfective maintenance
(iv) Preventive maintenance

(b) Define the term Audit. List its objectives. Also, discuss the responsibility of system auditor.
10

3. (a) Define an expert system. How are they different from traditional information systems? Explain various components of an expert system. Mention two examples of expert systems.
10

(b) Describe the criteria for form design and report designs.
10

4. (a) With reference to RDBMS, explain the use of the following files in-a system:
5x2=10
(i) Master file
(ii) Transaction file
(iii) Archive file
(iv) Audit file
(v) Work file

(b) How does a system analyst contribute to the success of a system?
10

5. Write short notes on the following:
4x5=20
(a) Prototype Approach
(b) Joint Application Development (JAD)
(c) SRS
(d) Decision Support Systems

MCS-014

MCA (Revised) / BCA (Revised)

Chapter 19: Term-End Examination, December, 2019

MCS-014: System Analysis and Design

Time: 3 Hours
Maximum Marks: 100
Weightage: 70

Note: (i) Question No. 1 is compulsory.
(ii) Answer any three Questions from the rest.

1. (a) List and explain all the components of a Management Information System.
10

(b) Describe the role of forms as means of input to the system and report as the means of output of the system with the
help of suitable examples for each.
10

(c) Discuss any two standards for documentation of software project.
10

(d) Draw DFD's upto 2nd-level for a Visitor's management system of a multinational company involved in manufacturing and sale of electronic products. Follow suitable conventions.
10

2. (a) Draw E-R diagram for "Visitor's Management System". Make necessary assumptions.
10

(b) Develop SRS for "Visitor's Management System". Make necessary assumptions.
10

3. (a) List and discuss the importance of various types of feasibility studies.
10

(b) Explain the process and technical related issues in software maintenance.
10

4. (a) Discuss the following types of testing techniques:
5x2=10
(i) Black Box testing
(ii) White Box testing

(b) Explain the criteria used for producing good reports.
10

5. Write short notes on the following:
4x5=20
(a) CASE tools
(b) Data dictionary
(c) Modularity
(d) Site Visits and Questionnaires

MCS-014
MCA (Revised) / BCA (Revised)
Chapter 20: Term-End Examination, June, 2020
MCS-014: System Analysis and Design

Time: 3 Hours
Maximum Marks: 100
Weightage: 70

Note: (i) Question No. 1 is compulsory.
(ii) Answer any three Questions from the rest.

1. (a) Draw a Data Flow Diagram (DFD) upto level-3 clearly showing various processes, data flow and data repositories for Doctor's appointment in a Hospital Management System. Make necessary assumptions.
10

(b) Write SRS outline for Doctor's Appointment in a Hospital Management System. Make necessary assumptions.
10

(c) Explain the tasks performed by a Systems Analyst.
10

(d) Explain how Waterfall model and Prototyping model can be accommodated in a spiral process model.
10

2. (a) What is JAD? What are its benefits and who are the key players? What are their roles?
6

(b) Give full form of CASE. Draw a CASE diagram showing all components. Explain each component briefly.
6

(c) Describe the characteristics of a good interface design. Describe the process of designing forms stating different steps
involved.
8

3. (a) Explain the different types of feasibility needed to be studies during software development.
10

(b) How can risks and threats to IT system be identified, analyzed and managed?
10

4. (a) What are the steps involved for designing a database. Explain using an example.
10

(b) What is modularity? How can it be achieved in Design? Explain the advantages of modular design.

1

0

5. Write short notes on the following: 5 x 4 =
20

(a) Data Dictionary
(b) Decision Support System
(c) Coupling
(d) Cost-Benefit Analysis

MCS-014
MCA (Revised) / BCA (Revised)
Chapter 21: Term-End Examination, February, 2021
MCS-014: System Analysis and Design

Time: 3 Hours
Maximum Marks: 100
Weightage: 70

Note: (i) Question No. 1 is compulsory.
(ii) Answer any three Questions from the rest.

1. (a) Draw a Data Flow Diagram (DFD) till level-3 depicting various processes, data flow and data repositories for booking a room in Hotel Management System. Make necessary assumptions.
10

(b) Draw an E-R Diagram for Hotel Management System. Make necessary assumptions.
10

(c) Write SRS outline for Hotel Management System. Make necessary assumptions.
10

(d) Explain the difference between ''Analysis'' and ''Design'' phases of Software Development.

10

2. (a) What is Data Dictionary? What are its uses? Explain with example.
8

(b) What is a Decision Table? Design a Decision Table for a system of your choice. Explain it.
8

(c) Describe any one method of performing Cost Benefit Analysis.
4

3. (a) Differentiate between Function-Oriented and Object-Oriented Design. Also explain the problems if two modules have high coupling.
8

(b) Explain the characteristics of MIS. Also list the components of MIS.
6

(c) Explain the criteria and specifications to be considered while designing Reports.
6

4. (a) Explain the process of design of physical records.
10

(b) Why is documentation needed during the development of a system? What are the various stages in SDLC where
documentation is required?
10

5. Write short notes on the following:
4x5=20

(a) Real Time and Distributed Systems
(b) Software Quality Assurance
(c) Types of File Organization
(d) Audit of Transaction

MCS-014
MCA (Revised) / BCA (Revised)
Chapter 22: Term-End Examination, June, 2021
MCS-014: System Analysis and Design

Time: 3 Hours
Maximum Marks: 100
Weightage: 70

Note: (i) Question No. 1 is compulsory.
(ii) Answer any three Questions from the rest.

1. (a) Draw DFD upto 2nd level (start from level-0) for a 'Library Information System'. Make necessary assumptions.
10

(b) Explain any *two* techniques for performing requirements analysis.
10

(c) Draw ERD for a 'Library Information System'. Make necessary assumptions.
10

(d) Explain different models of database design. Give examples.
10

2. (a) What is meant by CASE? Explain various components of CASE.
10

(b) What is meant by reverse engineering? What is meant by reengineering? How do they differ from each other?
10

3. (a) What are forms? Explain the process of design of forms.
10

(b) Is system maintenance essential? Explain different types of maintenance.
10

4. (a) Explain various types of file organization. What are the differences between a Master File and a Transaction File?
10

(b) What are inheritance and aggregation diagrams? Write differences between them.
10

5. (a) Explain various steps involved in the process of documentation.
10

(b) What is cohesion? Explain any four types of cohesion.
10

MCS-014
MCA (Revised) / BCA (Revised)
Chapter 23: Term-End Examination, December, 2021
MCS-014: System Analysis and Design

Time: 3 Hours
Maximum Marks: 100
Weightage: 70

Note: (i) Question No. 1 is compulsory.
(ii) Answer any three Questions from the rest.

1. (a) Draw DFDs up to 2nd level (start from Level-0) for a 'Hospital Information System'. Make necessary assumptions.
10

(b) Explain any two tasks that are performed during 'Design' phase of SDLC.
10

(c) Draw ERD for a 'Hospital Information System'. Make necessary assumptions.
10

(d) What is meant by 'Design Support System (DSS)'? Explain various components of it.
10

2. (a) What is meant by 'Feasibility Study'? Explain any two types of feasibility studies.
10

(b) Write SRS for a 'Hospital Information System'. Make necessary assumptions.
10

3. (a) What is meant by MIS? Explain any two functions of MIS in a business organisation.
10

(b) What is a Use Case Diagram? What is a Class Diagram? Explain with examples.
10

4. (a) Explain any two fact-finding techniques.
10

(b) What is the need for Concurrent Audit Techniques? Explain any four concurrent audit techniques.

1

0

5. (a) Explain any five criteria for design of reports.
10

(b) Explain the rules for naming Tables and Fields.
10

MCS-014
MCA (Revised) / BCA (Revised)
Chapter 24: Term-End Examination, June, 2022
MCS-014: System Analysis and Design

Time: 3 Hours
Maximum Marks: 100
Weightage: 70

Note: (i) Question No. 1 is compulsory.
(ii) Answer any three Questions from the rest.

1. (a) Draw DFDs upto 2nd level (start from level-O) for a 'Railway Reservation System'. Make necessary assumptions.
10

(b) Draw ERD for a Railway Reservation System. Make necessary assumptions.
10

(c) What are Visual CASE tools? Explain any *two* types of emerging CASE tools.
10

(d) What is an Expert System? Explain various components of an Expert System.
10

2. (a) Explain any two approaches for the development of Information Systems.
10

(b) Explain any two categories of skills that need to be possessed by a Systems Analyst.
10

3. (a) Explain the process of performing Cost- Benefit Analysis. Illustrate with an example.
10

(b) List and explain the Goals of Design.
10

4. (a) Explain any two types of Information with examples.
10

(b) What are various inputs to Physical Database Design? Also, list various guidelines for Database Design.
10

5. (a) Explain any two Computer Assisted Audit Techniques in detail.
10

(b) What is a Data Dictionary? How do System Analysts use Data Dictionaries? 10

MCS-014
MCA (Revised) / BCA (Revised)
Chapter 25: Term-End Examination, December, 2022
MCS-014: System Analysis and Design

Time: 3 Hours
Maximum Marks: 100
Weightage: 70

Note: (i) Question No. 1 is compulsory.
(ii) Answer any three Questions from the rest.

1. (a) What is a software system? Define SDLC. Should development of information system be considered as capital investment? Justify your answer.

10

(b) List and explain any two object-oriented CASE tools, with the help of suitable examples.
10

(c) What is a Form? How are forms designed? Briefly explain the criteria for form design.
10

(d) Explain why design principles are necessary for efficient software design. Differentiate between Top-down design
and Bottom-up approach of software design.
10

2. (a) Why is proper system analysis important for successful system development? Briefly explain the role of a system analyst in the overall system development.
10

(b) What is software maintenance? Explain adaptive maintenance and preventive maintenance, with examples.
10

3. (a) Explain ER Modelling, with an example. Also describe how ER Model is helpful in Database design.
10

(b) What is a Data Dictionary? Create a Data Dictionary for an ''Online Shopping System''. Make necessary assumptions.
10

4. (a) Prepare outline of SRS for an "Online Shopping System". Make necessary assumptions.
10

(b) What is an Expert System? What are its features? Explain the advantages and disadvantages of Expert Systems.

1

0

5. Write short notes on the following:

4x5=20

(a) Information Security
(b) Data Flow Diagram
(c) Transaction Processing System
(d) Quality of Software

MCS-014
MCA (Revised) / BCA (Revised)
Chapter 26: Term-End Examination, June, 2023
MCS-014: System Analysis and Design

Time: 3 Hours
Maximum Marks: 100
Weightage: 70

Note: (i) Question No. 1 is compulsory.
(ii) Answer any three Questions from the rest.

1. (a) What is Prototyping Approach for system design? Explain the steps involved in Prototyping process with the help of a diagram.

10

(b) What is a DFD? Draw DFD's upto 2nd level for "Online Examination System". Note: Make necessary assumptions.

1
0

(c) What is MIS? How is it useful for management control and strategic planning in an organization?

1
0

(d) What are CASE Tools? Explain the role of CASE Tools in technical and managerial aspects of software development process. List advantages and disadvantages of CASE Tools.

10

2. (a) Prepare an outline of SRS for an "Online Examination System". Make necessary assumptions.

1
0

(b) What are the duties of a systems analyst? Why technical and managerial skills are required for the job of systems analyst? Explain.

10

3. (a) What is the need of feasibility study? Explain any four issues involved in feasibility study.
10

(b) What is modularity in a system? Explain the concepts of coupling and cohesion. Is there any relationship between coupling and cohesion? Explain.

10

4. (a) Explain the following with an example for each:
2×5=10
(i) Class diagram
(ii) E-R diagram

(b) What is SDLC? Briefly explain all the seven phases of SDLC.
10

5. Write short notes on the following:
4×5=20
(a) Distributed Systems
(b) Structure Charts
(c) Internal and External Information
(d) Risk Analysis

MCS-014
MCA (Revised) / BCA (Revised)
Chapter 27: Term-End Examination, December, 2023
MCS-014: System Analysis and Design

Time: 3 Hours
Maximum Marks: 100
Weightage: 70

Note: (i) Question No. 1 is compulsory.
(ii) Answer any three Questions from the rest.

1. (a) Draw 0-level and 1-level DFDs for 'Student Admission System' of a university. Make necessary assumptions. 10

(b) Draw ERD for 'Student Admission System' of a university. Make necessary assumptions. 10

(c) Write SRS outline for 'Student Admission System' of a university. Make necessary assumptions. 10

(d) Explain any *two* fact finding techniques. Give their merits and demerits. 10

2. (a) Explain any *two* approaches for development of information systems. 10

(b) Why do businesses need system analysts? Explain the role of system analyst in modern business. 10

3. (a) Explain any *two* types of Documentation. 10

(b) Explain any *two* design principles using an example. 10

4. (a) What is a Data Dictionary? Explain any *two* process specification tools. 10

(b) Explain the process of designing forms and reports. 10

5. (a) What is a flat file? How does it differ from a database? Explain various steps in design of a database with the help of a diagram. 10

(b) Explain any *five* ways in which CASE tools can be used by an organization. 10

9 789369 723751

Printed at Repro India Ltd.